Reflections Through The Rain

KC Emery

India | USA | UK

Copyright © KC Emery
All Rights Reserved.

This book has been self-published with all reasonable efforts taken to make the material error-free by the author. No part of this book shall be used, reproduced in any manner whatsoever without written permission from the author, except in the case of brief quotations embodied in critical articles and reviews.

The Author of this book is solely responsible and liable for its content including but not limited to the views, representations, descriptions, statements, information, opinions, and references ["Content"]. The Content of this book shall not constitute or be construed or deemed to reflect the opinion or expression of the Publisher or Editor. Neither the Publisher nor Editor endorse or approve the Content of this book or guarantee the reliability, accuracy, or completeness of the Content published herein and do not make any representations or warranties of any kind, express or implied, including but not limited to the implied warranties of merchantability, fitness for a particular purpose.

The Publisher and Editor shall not be liable whatsoever...

Made with ❤ on the BookLeaf Publishing Platform
www.bookleafpub.in
www.bookleafpub.com

Dedication

This book is dedicated to so many people
who have had an impact on my life
in one way or another.

May you always remember:
You are Enough.
You are a living reflection of resilience and
a piece of the infinite masterpiece called life.

Preface

This is a collection of sonnets, villanelles,
lyrical, and free verse poetry
for those who have ever felt like too much,
not enough, or lost somewhere in between.

It is about carrying quiet battles,
learning to pause, reflect, and try again.
It is about searching for clarity in the fog,
and being brave enough to sit with it long enough
to let it change you for the better.

This book is also a thank you for the listeners,
the friends and family who make space for others,
and for themselves, even when it's hard.
I hope you find something in this collection
that make you feel seen too.

That's the thing about feelings:
they're meant to be felt.
So if any of these poems stir something in you,
then we've met in that space
where being human is enough.
We're all connected in more ways than we realize.

Acknowledgements

To my family and friends:
Thank you for your love, patience,
and belief in me, even when I doubt myself.
Your support has been the foundation on which
I've built both my healing and my art.

To my professors and mentors:
Thank you for challenging me,
nurturing my curiosity,
and encouraging me to look deeper
into the meaning behind my words.

And to the authors, poets,
and storytellers who came before me:
Thank you for reminding me of the power
of language and the courage it takes to share it.
Your words gave me permission to find my own.

This book exists because of each of you.

1. Holding Still

I used to think kindness meant reaching,
to steady every shaking hand,
to gather every dropped piece of someone else's world.
I called it love, though it hollowed me out quietly,
like water smoothing a stone that never asked to shine.
I could read their pain before they spoke it,
their smallest flinch, the swallowed sigh,
a language of ache I was fluent in.
And still, knowing didn't mean saving,
not when saving meant sinking too.

I'm learned, slowly,
that love isn't sacrifice when it's measured,
that balance is the quiet refusal to drown.

So you start to let the water fall away,
hold your palms open but not cupped,
watch the ache pass through without keeping it.

Finding a balance in my reflection,
is it's own sort of kindness:
to stay afloat, yet still be warm.

2. Letter Unopened

The mail arrives, another poisoned page,
your scrawl still trembles with unspent decay.
I feel the ghost of all that brittle rage,
but learned to set fire to it anyway.

Once, I absorbed those storms, became their shore,
let every wave of guilt erode my name.
You never asked if I could carry more,
just hurled your hurt and called it mine to claim.

Now silence is my answer, calm and wide,
a stillness you mistake for cold retreat.
It burns you that I will not step inside
the chaos where you still find your seat.

I know it is heavy, that unowned pain,
until you face it, it will be your chain.

3. The Fixer

I held the shards she shattered on the floor,
I masked her lies until they bled in me,
too young to save, I could endure no more.

Each gift I gave became a sharpened sore,
each act of love returned in cruelty,
I held the shards she shattered on the floor.

Her shadow fed on every open door,
her voice a cage I could not break free,
too young to save, I could endure no more.

The world she broke was never mine to store,
I turned away, and chose my own decree,
I held the shards she shattered on the floor,
too young to save, I could endure no more.

4. Finding Her

She spent her life in borrowed skin,
becoming what they needed then.
A chameleon in every room,
she danced around her silent doom.

She learned to smile, to keep the peace,
to silence storms and seek release.
But piece by piece, she came undone
a stranger forged from everyone.

One day she woke and couldn't trace
the girl beneath the borrowed face.
But now, through cracks where pain once bled,
she's finding pieces she had shed.

She once was fire, soft and wild,
a dreamer, poet, stubborn child.
She's breathing life into that flame,
and slowly, she recalls her name.

5. No is Enough

No.
No is enough.
I do not owe you explanation.
I built these walls.
They are thick.
They are mine.
You reach.
You claw.
Your voice used to map my veins.
Not anymore.
Not mine to reroute.

I love.
But love has a line.
A fence.
A gate I close.
No guilt.
No bending.
No apology.

No.
All of it.
Deserved.

6. The Yes I Keep

I used to scatter myself like seeds
in a wind that didn't ask for them,
hoping someone, anyone,
would bloom from my effort.
I said yes to things that hollowed me,
to voices that whispered "you should"
until my own heartbeat became a stranger.
No more.
I am learning that my peace
is not a gift to be negotiated,
nor a currency to be spent
on the approval of others.
I am learning that saying no is not cruelty,
but an act of preservation,
a quiet reclaiming of the territory
that is mine alone.
I do not owe anyone a single breath I haven't chosen.
I do not owe anyone the surrender of my calm.
I say yes to the stillness that feeds me,
to the moments that make me whole,
to the life that grows only when I guard it,
only when I am enough without the weight
of other people's expectations.

7. Cracks in my Wall

I build my walls like riverbanks,
steady, unyielding, holding back old floods.

But walls that never bend
trap the still water too,
and the pond inside turns cold.

So I leave a crack,
a shimmer on the surface,
light and warmth spilling in
without letting the storm break through.

I watch my reflection pulse,
feel the water move with connection,
ready to seal the breach if needed.

8. Ashes or Fire

They smiled.
Sharp teeth hidden behind words
that cut deeper than knives.
Used me.
Tossed me.
Pretended we were friends.
I learned fast: trust is a luxury
Fake hands grab, twist, and vanish.

But then,
A hand reaches before I even fall.
A voice that says,
"I see you. You're not alone."
Not for gain. Not for applause.
Just real. Just steady.
Fake friends burn.
True friends light.

And I?
I finally know the difference.

9. Warded

They weave their whispers in the crowded air,
a tangle meant to cloud what's truly known.
Their eyes are empty, and their hearts unfair,
yet seek to dim the light that I have shown.

For when their own reflections hold no grace,
they cast their shadows outward, sharp and sly.
No merit guides the words they dare embrace,
but jealousy that blinds them as they lie.

Yet I remain, unmoved by petty spite,
for curiosity's spark cannot be chained.
Their twisting tongues cannot eclipse my light,
nor stain the truth that I have earned and gained.

So let them speak; their envy feeds my flame,
the more they try, the stronger burns my name.

10. Sleepwalkers

You built a world of falsehoods you called true,
we begged, we reasoned,
our truths ignored each day,
blind to the patterns only we could show.

You followed what you were told,
never questioning,
free?,
while we climbed higher,
tracing maps you brushed away,
you built a world of falsehoods you called true.

Our voices rose, our logic burned,
yet you shrugged,
critical minds wasted on walls you'd never sway,
blind to the patterns only we could show,
you built a world of falsehoods you called true.

11. Loops

Life runs on loops, whatever vibe you send
will circle back and shape the days you see.
When you build others up, that light won't end;
it finds its way back home eventually.

The world reflects the focus that you give,
feed peace, you'll feel it; feed the fight, you'll burn.
You choose what kind of stories you let live,
what scenes you skip, what lessons you return.

The drama's always playing, loud and near,
but you don't have to watch or take the bait.
Protect your calm, stay grounded, clear, sincere,
good energy will meet you in your state.

So send out love, not noise, not empty show,
what you support is what will start to grow.

12. Quiet Ones

In quiet rooms, the towers rise,
spines stacked like sentinels in the dark.
Whispers slip between shelves,
an alphabet army mustering unseen.

You clip a page; we plant seeds.
Roots tangle beneath your fences,
branches scrape the sky where rules fall short.
Eyes open, small hands reach,
a tide learns the shape of resistance.

Ink breathes where silence feared to tread.
Walls of paper, walls of thought,
your shadow cannot linger here.

We move like wind in the stacks,
a reckoning written in margins.
Every ban fans the fire,
and the quiet ones are never truly quiet.

13. Truth Matters

I knew him once before the world took note,
before the songs, before the lights and fame;
He laughed like summer, and rocked the boat,
a truth so real, no one dared take aim.

He never tried to fit where others would land,
he lived his way, unshaken, wild, and kind;
and just by being him, he took a stand,
and taught me not to leave myself behind.

When voices rose to judge what they don't know,
he faced them all with quiet, steady grace.
Even if pain or haters appeared in places he'd go,
his artistry shut down every negative space.

One day he might forget the friend I used to be,
but he's a big reason I had the courage to just be me.

14. But Summer

They say it's not a hard job.
They don't deserve more pay,
they should stop complaining,
educators get summers off, after all.
As if two months of sunlight
can thaw the cold that builds from endless battles
fought quietly behind classroom doors.
They don't see the policies that protect the cruel
and punish the kind, the meetings laced with lies.
They don't know the exhaustion
of holding hope and giving until they vanish
because no one funds the fix.
They don't hear the parents with pitchforks,
the gossip turned into war cries,
the leaders who rule through fear.
They just see the crafts, the smiles,
not the tears behind them.
They count "time off,"
not the hours spent rebuilding
what the system keeps breaking.
So yes, educators have summers off.
Time to grieve what the year took,
to piece themselves together
just enough to walk back into the fire again.

15. Regret

I tossed the same weights I carried onto you,
not knowing they were mine to unpack,
not knowing pain is learned before it's healed.
I judged, I tried to control,
I said things that cut deeper than I realized,
because I didn't yet know my own scars.

Now I look back and it hurts,
how unfair it was to make you the mirror
for what I hadn't faced in myself.
I would rewind, I would apologize
to every quiet moment I disturbed,
every trust I bent under my ignorance.

But I learned.
And for that, I am grateful.
Even regret has a place when it teaches me
how to hold the world, and myself,
with gentler hands.

16. Staircase Leaps

He built his world from grit and open skies,
with hands that shaped a dream no man could steal.
Each loss he bore just made his spirit rise,
a southern heart of iron wrapped in steel.

Through savant and sage, he carved his rightful place,
a self-made man who never lost his way.
Yet still, he'd trade it all to see my face,
light up with joy at dusk's soft golden ray.

I'd leap to him from staircases so wide,
no fear, just knowing he would catch me whole.
His arms, a place where love and trust collide,
where I could rest my heart, my dreams, my soul.

He taught me how to rise when I am small,
and that he'd catch me, always, through it all.

17. Tidal Treasures

The shore stretched wide beneath the sky,
a travel park where young dreams could fly.
My grandparents walked the morning sand,
time itself held in their hands.

Papaw's detector hummed and gleamed,
each buried coin a hope redeemed.
While I bent low where tide foam curled,
to find some treasures of this world.

Strangers' voices drifted near,
friends from places far and clear.
No fences stood, no clocks to chase,
just sun and salt, an endless space.

I didn't know, as daylight burned,
that freedom's shape was being learned.
Those days remain, both calm and rife,
as some of the best days of my life.

18. My Pirate

Ahoy! he'd cry, and plant himself with flair,
"This old leg? Just a stool for me to share!"
The children stared, wide-eyed, in pure delight,
"Did he chop it off?" they'd whisper in fright.

A patch, a hat, a grin that could light the skies,
stories like treasures danced behind his eyes.
Summers with him were maps of laughter and sun,
where lessons and mischief melted into one.

Now winds carry whispers only I can hear,
a nudge, a wink, a voice that steers me clear.
Though he's sailed beyond where mortal eyes roam,
his compass points me straight, I'm never alone.

So here's to Papaw, pirate, teacher, friend,
his love and laughter chart my course till the end.

19. Keeper Of Grace

You've always shown us love without condition,
a steady hand when choices felt unsure.
Even when we stumbled, your intuition
saw our hearts, and your grace made them secure.

You noticed bitterness and didn't join it,
but offered kindness where shadows had grown.
The lost, the weary, the ones who'd been pointed,
you lifted them with a love all your own.

Through thick and thin and Papaw by your side,
you hold every memory like a flame.
A quiet hero, our family's guide,
you taught us love is stronger than any pain.

I love you more than words will ever show,
the force of good that helped our family grow.

20. Smiling

He left before the story felt complete,
yet his voice still hums in the quiet,
the low whistle of wind through old oaks,
the laughter that lifts from familiar rooms.
Once a wild flame, he learned by burning,
and prayed his sons might find gentler fires.
He saw himself in their sharp grins,
their restless eyes, the way they dared the world.

Now he lives in every small gesture,
a hand smoothing soil into order,
a child's footsteps echoing through his house,
paint smeared across a traveler's sleeve.
One son shapes earth into beauty,
roots deep where his father once dreamed.
The other catches light, turns it to color,
chasing wonder across mountains and seas.

He isn't gone, only scattered,
in their laughter, their craft, their kindness.
You can see him in them, and he is smiling.

21. Creature Keeper

Upon her land, where dawn and hoofbeats blend,
She walks - rough-handed, gentle in command;
each beast that wanders knows it's found a friend,
a refuge built by care and weathered hand.

Her stables hum with breath and steady heart,
the dogs like shadows guard her every stride;
In kitchen bowls the neon fishes dart,
while wings in office corners sing and glide.

The den hums soft, small paws in swirling play,
her laughter, low, reshapes the wild to tame;
like sire before, she meets the wolf halfway,
and leaves it peaceful, never quite the same.

Fierce guardian soul, through rugged grace known,
she loves all life as if it were her own.

22. Wide World

In Virginia's mountains, the world grew wide,
beyond the small town where she'd longed to hide.
Deer nibbled apples beneath sky so blue,
foxes schemed in the hen house - oh, who knew?

She learned that dirt beneath her nails was art,
planting vegetables straight from the heart.
Through creeks she stumbled, slipped on stones,
chasing the dogs with wild, laughing tones.

Rooster calls woke her to dawn's soft light,
candlelit evenings closed the night.
Tractors rumbled, love was tough,
yet every lesson shaped her enough.

A place of growth, of freedom, of play,
of simple joys that would never decay.
Mountains and people etched deep in her soul,
a childhood that made her entirely whole.

23. Quiet Chain

I still remember her, the first to stand,
to name her love and take their scorned reply.
They cast her out with trembling, holy hands,
and we were taught that truth could make you die.

So we grew careful, quiet as the night,
hiding our colors under borrowed skin;
we learned to nod, to keep the edges tight,
to love in whispers, never to begin.

But now I see the youngest blaze their name,
their laughter rings where silence used to stay;
they live unshamed, unsoftened by the blame,
and light the paths we lost along the way.

I watch with pride, as they set us all free;
breaking the quiet chain courageously.

24. Railroad Ties

Every Christmas,
same game, same split.
Men's gifts. Women's gifts.
Two piles, two different worlds.

The guys always got knives,
handmade from railroad ties,
by an uncle's steady hand,
shining like a mirror.

I wanted one.
But " knives are men's gifts," they said.
"Choose something nice."
So I smiled and unwrapped
something soft,
something that wasn't me.

Now he's gone,
and I wish I'd broken the rules,
because who says
what's meant for who?
Girls can use knives too.

25. Just Love

She didn't give birth, but she gave me her time,
her patience, her heart, her effort - sublime.

No lectures or guilt, just showing she'll stay,
a love that sticks around when others go away.

She cheered me on, even when I fell flat,
forgave every mood swing and teenage spat.

She taught me that family is more than a name,
it's kindness and showing up, always the same.

So here's to you, bonus moms sent from above,
no "step" is required when you lead with love.

26. Bond Beyond

Through rushing rapids, laughter's echo flies,
at waterfalls, their joy cascades in song;
From theme parks' lights to ruins where time lies,
their friendship: steady, deep, and ever strong.

They soared through clouds - first flights, first dreams to chase,
embraced old friends in cities far and wide;
At games and festivals, the crowds, the grace,
each stood as anchor, heart, and trusted guide.

Though distance calls, and life must have its say,
their paths diverge like rivers to the sea;
yet in the storm, when skies are torn away,
their bond holds fast - unbroken, endlessly.

For roots once twined in laughter's golden thread,
will bloom anew, no matter where they're led.

S.H.

27. Mosaic of Us

You lived downstairs, a quiet mystery,
and I was lonely, lost inside my head.
One day I asked if you'd make art with me,
a mosaic bloomed where silence used to spread.

We talked through tiles, through color, glue, and mess,
through heartbreaks, wild nights, and fated loves.
Each year stitched stories neither could have guessed,
yet we weathered every storm's greatest shoves.

Now you're building life with little hands to hold,
and I watch you shine, so steady, kind, and true.
I've seen your courage turn to something gold,
and I'm just proud to still be there for you.

From bits, we've built friendship that never dies,
a lifetime of laughing through lows and highs.

M.G.

28. Trauma Club

Alone I walked through shadowed halls,
where echoes of my childhood calls.
The weight of wounds too deep to name,
a silent fire, a private flame.

Then came the souls who'd fought the same,
their scars like mine, their hearts aflame.
In whispered words and knowing eyes,
we found the truth beneath the lies.

Some chose to leave, their pain too wide,
we honor them, though still we stride.
Together here, we mend, we rise,
a shared embrace, a soft reprise.

For power grows when hearts unite,
and love can light the darkest night.
What was stolen, we reclaim,
through care, through voice, trying not to blame.

29. Pogue

Beneath tall trees, the sunlight drifts like gold,
The air smells sweet of petals, damp with dew,
A hidden garden whispers tales untold.
Vines twist above, a lattice green and bold,
Shadows dance softly, hiding the city view,
Beneath tall trees, the sunlight drifts like gold.

Roses bleed colors no eye could behold,
Some blushing pinks, some crimsons kissed with blue,
A hidden garden whispers tales untold.
We lay our blanket where the soft moss folds,
To-go sushi shared, the world outside feels untrue,
Beneath tall trees, the sunlight drifts like gold.

A Shakespearean stage looms, its stone grown old,
Yet here, laughter echoes where only we pursue,
A hidden garden whispers tales untold.
Moments bloom like flowers, fragile yet bold,
Escaping rush and duty, in our secret pew,
Beneath tall trees, the sunlight drifts like gold,
A hidden garden whispers tales untold.

30. Dance Defense

We twirl and spin with laughter in our hair,
our sneakers stomping without a single care.
We pick our spots with ninja-like finesse,
avoiding creeps and their awkward "hey, yes?"

A circle here, a line over there,
a cleverly chosen corner for flair.
Yet somehow, some guys appear anyway,
as if "no thanks" is a new word they can't say.

We plot our exits like spies on a mission,
back-up plans ready with tactical precision.
We travel in squads, a synchronized crew,
because "leave me alone" doesn't always get through.

Still, we dance, we laugh, we claim our space,
dodging the clueless with style and grace.
A victory dance with our witty retreat,
in groups we move, because safety is sweet.

31. Friend I Needed

She walks with light that doesn't seek the fame,
yet brightens every soul along her way.
A gentle strength, too humble to name,
but felt in all she does, in what she'll say.

She lifts the lost with just a steady glance,
believes in hearts the world forgets to see.
Where others pause, she dares to take the chance,
to shape a life, to help someone feel free.

Her hands raise children, not just through the years,
but with a love that makes their small world grow.
And still she turns and calms adult-born fears,
with kindness only rare hearts ever show.

She's a gift to the world I'm glad I know,
a friend I'm proud of wherever I go.

K.H.

32. Dance Princess

In a studio of mirrors and dreams,
Princess Beth taught more than dance.
Through every plié, leap, and song,
she showed us how to take a chance.

She taught us to stumble with grace,
to sparkle beneath the stage's light,
to lift each other through the turns,
and keep on trying 'til it's right.

She made us proud to be ourselves,
to stand tall and be a go-getter.
She reminded us, with a knowing smile,
that anything boys could do, we could do better.

Her lessons weren't just steps or moves,
but courage, kindness, poise, and heart,
and though the music fades away,
her rhythm and lessons remain in every part.

Once little girls who danced and twirled,
are now "Betharina's" spread across the world.

33. Diversity

A family stitched from many hearts and lands,
they showed me love can grow where differences meet.
Each story shared, a treasure in our hands.

Through open doors and warmly offered plans,
I learned that every soul brings something sweet.
A family stitched from many hearts and lands.

They welcomed one who journeyed from strange sands,
and made a place where every voice is complete.
Each story shared, a treasure in our hands.

To know someone, to truly understand,
is to find a harmony both bright and fleet.
A family stitched from many hearts and lands,
each story shared, a treasure in our hands.

T.S.F

34. Community

When winds tore roofs and rivers claimed the streets,
the world seemed fragile, chaos uncontained.
Yet hearts aligned where need and courage meets,
and neighbors rose, though fear and loss remained.

With hands that carried food and blankets warm,
they wove a safety net from care and grit.
No hero cloaked in fame, no perfect form,
just ordinary souls refusing to quit.

Through shattered doors,
through rain that soaked the ground,
they brought each other light where darkness fell.
A thousand voices joined without a sound,
a symphony of love that none could quell.

The storm destroyed, yet human hearts restored,
in unity, they found our own reward.

Helene '24

35. Shame vs. Guilt

Shame whispers softly, "You are not enough,"
Its weight feels endless, its tone always tough.
It blankets the heart in a shadowed night,
turning our flaws into shameful blight.

Guilt, by contrast, points to a deed,
A choice, a moment, a misplanted seed.
It says, "You acted, and now you can mend,"
A teacher, a guide, a chance to amend.

Shame says, "You're broken, forever confined,"
Guilt says, "Reflect, and be gentle, be kind."
One crushes the soul, the other can steer,
one traps in fear, the other clears.

To know the difference is freedom, is light,
to hold guilt with care, and not shame in fright.
For guilt can guide us to repair and to grow,
while shame only teaches us what not to show.

36. Worry is a Prayer

Worry is a quiet prayer for the worst,
a summon of storms we don't want to see.
Every "what if" feeds the fear, the curse,
and locks our future in a dark decree.

But imagine the best, even for a while,
picture the doors that could open wide.
The mind will shape the world in its own style,
so why let fear decide the tide?

Don't plant doubts in the garden of your days,
water hope instead and watch it grow.
Thoughts become seeds; your mind paves the ways
to the life you choose, not the life of woe.

Worry less, dream more, let your heart steer,
the future bends to what you hold most dear.

37. Awaken

Return, return, oh sleeping flame,
through shadowed nights and whispered name.
Through lives repeated, round and round,
the lesson waits where truth is found.

Awake, awake, oh wandering heart,
from veils of fear, let self depart.
The mirror waits, the stillness calls,
through rising tides and silent falls.

See, see, the path that spirals near,
through pain, through loss, through love, through fear.
The seed is planted, the soul may grow,
the light will find the one who seeks to know.

One day, one breath, one tender glance,
the cycle bends, the soul shall dance.
Return, return, oh sleeping flame,
and walk at last in your own name.

38. No Ledger

Love because it feels like sunlight in your chest,
don't let your hurt spill onto someone else.
Simply loving is its own return.
Your pain is yours, leave no mess behind,
no one should carry what you choose to lose.
Love because it feels like sunlight in your chest.
the world is rough, hearts get compressed,
Small acts of care can shift the blues.
simply loving is its own return.

A smile, a hand, a word, a moment blessed,
these gifts ask nothing, take no excuse.
love because it feels like sunlight in your chest.
Anger fades if you give it rest,
let tenderness decide the path you cruise.
simply loving is its own return.
Every choice counts, be mindful, not possessed,
healing others starts with what you choose.
Love because it feels like sunlight in your chest,
simply loving is its own return.

39. Evolving

I am grateful
for the lessons that cracked me open,
for the ones that broke little pieces of me
so I could stretch wider, hold more, see deeper.

Grateful for the people who handed me those lessons
even when they cut sharp,
and for the ones who stayed
to help me sweep up the fragments
I scattered on the floors of my own making.

Grateful for patience,
for grace given when I fumbled through territories
no one else had the courage to tread.

For the guidance of those who know more,
who have walked paths I could only follow in awe.

I am grateful for the exposure,
for the moments that shaped me without my asking,
for every chance to witness
the vastness of life and be molded by it.

I am grateful for what I have,

even as I see that true reward has nothing to do with things.

Love, understanding,
and growth - these are my treasures.
I am a work in progress, and that is enough.

Because I chose movement, change,
and the refusal to linger in the shadows of who I once was.

I am grateful.
For the cracks,
for the light between them,
and for the journey itself.

40. Love Your Story

You can't hug yourself
if you scowl at the past,
or blame every stumble,
each fall that didn't last.
Those trips and those flops,
those awkward mistakes,
are the sprinkles and frosting
that life sometimes bakes.
The bruise on your knee,
the tears that you cried,
The nights you felt lost
or tried hard and sighed,

All stitched into you,
like stars in a quilt,
Each thread of your story,
both joy and guilt.
So dance with your scars,
let your heart give a grin,
Thank every wrong turn
for the strength found within.
To love who you are,
you must nod and agree:
You're the sum of it all, your whole history!

www.ingramcontent.com/pod-product-compliance
Lightning Source LLC
Chambersburg PA
CBHW070039070426
42449CB00012BA/3101